LET'S LEARN ABOUT
NATURAL RESOURCES

FOSSIL FUELS

Jill Sherman

Enslow Publishing
101 W. 23rd Street
Suite 240
New York, NY 10011
USA

enslow.com

Words to Know

energy The ability to do work.

fossil fuel A fuel formed in the earth from dead plants and animals.

natural gas Gas that comes from the earth's crust.

natural resource Something from nature that people use.

nonrenewable Describing something that cannot be replenished.

pollution Damage to the earth.

CONTENTS

Fuel for Our World

Flip on a light. Ride on the bus. Turn on the heat. All these things use **energy**. That energy likely comes from **fossil fuels**.

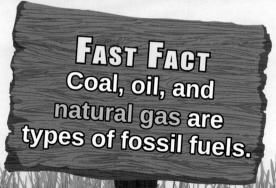

FAST FACT
Coal, oil, and natural gas are types of fossil fuels.

From the Earth

Fossil fuels are a **natural resource**. They come from the earth. We use the earth's natural resources to make new things. Everything around us came from the earth in some way.

FAST FACT
Other natural resources are water, soil, air, plants, and animals.

Making Energy

Fossil fuels go into our cars and trucks. The engine burns the fuel. It creates energy. Now the car can go.

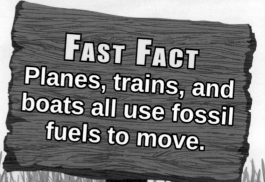

FAST FACT
Planes, trains, and boats all use fossil fuels to move.

Electrical Energy

Electricity is a kind of energy. We make it in power plants. Power plants burn coal. Some burn natural gas. The plant turns this energy into electricity.

FAST FACT
Fossil fuels are a nonrenewable resource. Once they are used up, they are gone forever.

Everyday Energy

We use fuels at home, too. They heat our homes. They also cook our food. Inside, we use them to roast dinner. Outside, we use them to grill burgers.

Making Things

Do you use some things made of plastic? A bounce house? A lunch box? A toothbrush? Plastic comes from fossil fuels.

Fossil Fuels All Around

What else is made from fossil fuels? Your clothes or bike helmet may have fabric made from fossil fuels. Fossil fuels are in the ink on our money. And they are in the asphalt of our roads.

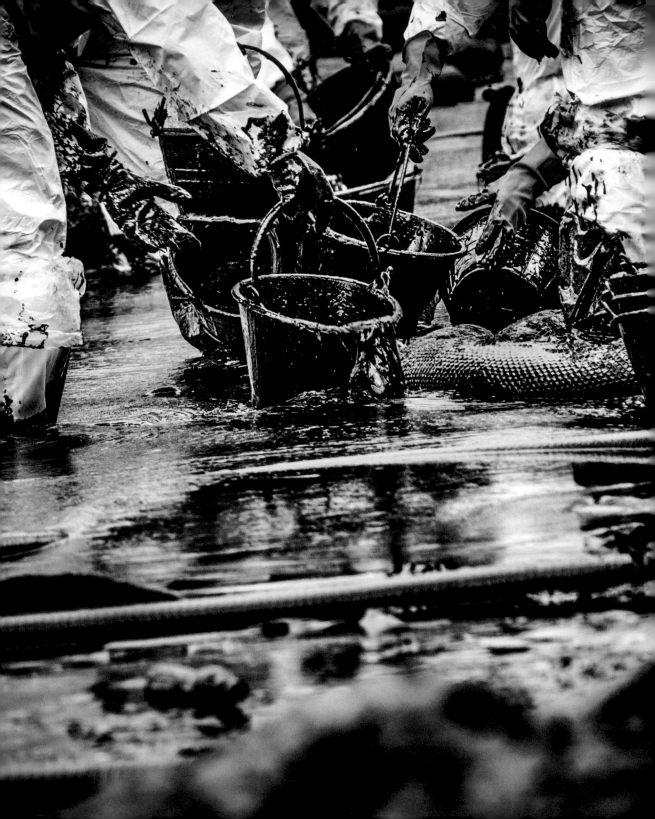

Risky Business

Fossil fuels can harm the earth. Coal mining strips the land of plants. Oil spills poison the water. Burning fossil fuels causes **pollution**.

FAST FACT
Pollution makes the air dirty and unsafe to breathe. It makes water unsafe for people and animals.

What You Can Do

To save energy, burn fewer fossil fuels. Turn off lights. Walk to school. Small steps make a big difference.

FAST FACT

Not all power comes from fossil fuels. The sun, wind, and water can be used for energy. These are renewable and cleaner sources of energy.

Activity

Fossil Fuel Formation

MATERIALS

leaves   clear
twigs   plastic
sand   cup
water

Fossil fuels are formed from decayed plants and animals. They were covered by earth for millions of years. The pressure changed them. Make a miniature version of this process to see how it might work.

Procedure:

1. Spread a layer of sand on the bottom of the container and cover with a few inches of water.

2. Place leaves and twigs in the water.

3. Let the container sit for two weeks. Then record your observations.

4. Pour another layer of sand on top of the leaves and twigs. What happens?

5. Now, pour off the excess water. Which layer do you think would turn into coal if it sat long enough?

6. Let the container sit for a few more days. Has it changed? Do you think this is like the way fossils were formed over time?

LEARN MORE

Books

Bang, Molly. *Buried Sunlight: How Fossil Fuels Have Changed the Earth*. New York, NY: The Blue Sky Press, 2014.

Hansen, Amy S. *Fossil Fuels: Buried in the Earth*. New York, NY: Power Kids Press, 2010.

Rice, William B. *The Story of Fossil Fuels*. Huntington Beach, CA: Teacher Created Materials, 2015.

Websites

Energy Kids
eia.gov/kids
Find information about energy sources and the history of energy, along with fun, educational games.

Energy Star
energystar.gov/index.cfm?c=kids.kids_index
Discover different types of energy and explore the ways you can save our planet by becoming energy efficient.

INDEX

Published in 2018 by Enslow Publishing, LLC.
101 W. 23rd Street, Suite 240, New York, NY 10011

Copyright © 2018 by Enslow Publishing, LLC.

Library of Congress Cataloging-in-Publication Data

Names: Sherman, Jill, author.
Title: Fossil fuels / Jill Sherman.
Description: New York : Enslow Publishing, 2018. | Series: Let's learn about natural resources | Includes bibliographical references and index.
Identifiers: LCCN 2017018166| ISBN 9780766092365 (library bound) | ISBN 9780766091511 (pbk.) | ISBN 9780766093829 (6 pack)
Subjects: LCSH: Fossil fuels—Juvenile literature. | Energy industries—Juvenile literature.
Classification: LCC TP318.3 .S43 2018 | DDC 333.8/2—dc23

LC record available at https://lccn.loc.gov/2017018166

Printed in China

To Our Readers: We have done our best to make sure all website addresses in this book were active and appropriate when we went to press. However, the author and the publisher have no control over and assume no liability for the material available on those websites or on any websites they may link to. Any comments or suggestions can be sent by email to customerservice@enslow.com.

Photo Credits: Cover, p. 1 Robb Kendrick/National Geographic Magazine/Getty Images; interior pages background Andrey_Kuzmin/Shutterstock.com; p. 4 BlueOrange Studio/Shutterstock.com; p. 6 NPeter/Shutterstock.com; p. 8 egd/Shutterstock.com; p. 10 Maureen Perez/Shutterstock.com; p. 12 LightField Studios/Shutterstock.com; p. 14 Brocreative/Shutterstock.com; p. 16 Kdonmuang/Shutterstock.com; p. 18 Tigergallery/Shutterstock.com; p. 20 Andy Dean Photography/Shutterstock.com.